To You

Aayushi Srinivasan

BookLeaf Publishing

India | USA | UK

Made with ❤ on the BookLeaf Publishing Platform
www.bookleafpub.in
www.bookleafpub.com

Dedication

To the life experiences that have shaped me—especially my journey as a Fauji kid—I am deeply grateful.

To my mother and father, whose patience and belief in me have been the bedrock of my strength.

To my sister, my unwavering support through every challenge, and to my brother-in-law, the ever-optimistic soul.

To my two brothers and their wives—you have all been quiet, steady constants in my life.

To my friends—you know who you are. <3 <3

And to you, the readers, who may find pieces of your own story in mine, here at the age of 29.

This book is dedicated to You.

Preface

I've always turned to poetry—scribbling verses into Keep Notes and scattered notebooks over the years—as a quiet way of making sense of the world around me.
This book of poems began as part of a writing challenge with BookLeaf Publishing, but what started as a simple prompt soon blossomed into something far more personal.
Through this journey, I rediscovered my love for poetry—an art form I once believed I had left behind in childhood. With every poem, I found myself reconnecting with emotions, memories, and moments I thought were long forgotten.
This collection isn't just a compilation of poems; it's a reflection of growth, healing, and rediscovery. It represents the quiet, constant thread of writing that's always been with me, even when I wasn't fully aware of it.
Thank you for walking with me through this journey.

Acknowledgements

First and foremost, I would like to express my deepest gratitude to BookLeaf Publishing for offering me the opportunity to participate in their writing challenge. This journey has not only reignited my passion for poetry but has also allowed me to rediscover myself in ways I hadn't imagined.

I owe a special thank you to my family—my mother, whose unwavering patience and love have been my constant support; my father, whose belief in me remains a guiding force from beyond this world; and my sister, whose strength and unconditional support have been the foundation upon which I stand. *(I could not have made that cover page without your inputs!)* Without them, none of this would have been possible.

To all the experiences and memories that shaped the words within these pages, thank you for teaching me more than I could have learned from any classroom.

Lastly, I would like to thank every reader who has taken the time to journey with and through these poems. Your presence here makes this journey even more meaningful. I hope you could resonate with some part of these anthology of poems.

1. Drown, Tsunami 2004

Breathe in slow,
Hold, don't let go—
Then release with quiet dread.
"Are you not scared we're all dead!!??"
A voice on the Reliance handset.

December winds and chill,
As the coast stood still,
TVs blared with breaking cries
As Chennai stood, swallowed by the tide
A few left, with tears to hide.

The ocean roared
Choppers soared
But silence gripped the sand
A hundred thousand souls, lost;
With no time to understand

Glug glug glug -
I drank and stared

My 8 year old eyes wide,
with much despair
News poured in - "Over 200,000 lives lost",
with none prepared
As death had no disguise to wear.

A sea of loss
A sea of cries
It came with vengeance,
And left like the wail of *kadalamma* denied
A memory etched, of vanishing light

And in the silence of what remained
A day after Christmas
and Winds blowing unchained -
Was grief, water and names unnamed.

Note: *Kadalamma or "Mother of the Sea" is a revered figure amongst the coastal communities of Kerala and parts of Tamil Nadu. In these communities, the sea is personified as nurturing yet formidable mother goddess.*

2. Smells Like -

The rain taps soft against the glass,
while puddles form in the grass.
The smell of earth is fresh and sweet,
I wrap a blanket 'round me,
The hissing of the kettle and grinding coffee,
as the joy begins to slowly simmer—
We're having soupy ramen for dinner!

3. A Naval Lieutenant

There's something about you, friend—
that momentarily reminds me of him,
a retired Commander named *Tinku Vasan*,
like a warship,
steady and strong,
holding my hand at graduation,
standing proud,
never spreading himself too thin.
Is it the smile,
or the aura—
that of a Lieutenant?
Or perhaps the calm,
composed grin,
that breaks the ice
paper-thin?
I dunno, man—
but it's definitely not
the height,
or the gin.

4. Fauj Hai, Mauj Nahi

(A poem for every station left behind)

"Chalo, let's pack."
We've been transferred again.
"So soon?"—asks Amma,
her voice laced with a sigh,
"But we've been here for only over a year!";
A rhetoric, where she knows the drill;
as the familiar B-type quarters
buzz with a whirr of boxes, goodbyes and new thrills.
My little toe knows the wall
at the bedroom corner—
the one I always stubbed it on.
Funny, the things we grow to love
right before we leave them.
"Where to next?"
Vizag.
"When does the truck come?"
In two days.
That's all the time we have—

to fold our lives into cardboard,
to tape spoons, cutlery and memories into a box,
to shut the tiny, humble kitchen
that once felt like a world.
To say goodbye—
to friends who will walk the same school corridors
long after we're gone,
till maybe, just maybe,
we meet again at some distant station
where names have changed, and faces, grown.
But with a quiet familiarity
That never quite left.
Private phones weren't much in the 2000s—
just whispers of a future.
So when someone knocked on our cluttered door
with hot food in hand,
we welcomed more than the belonging—
We welcomed impromptu dinners and warmth.

We learned the art of small adjustments:
not wearing our favorite clothes
because they were already packed,
leaving behind best friends
without phone numbers,
only memories,
because they might be transferred too—
and we'd never know where.

So we stood,
by doors half-closed,
hearts half-packed,
trying not to cry
as the train once more, left on track.
And through it all,
a steady voice smiled and said—
"Fauj hai, mauj nahi."
This is the life we're given—
not for ease,
but for honor.

Note: The words Fauj and Mauj have their origins in
Persian/Arabic commonly adopted into Hindi/Urdu.
Fauj - *meaning: army or military.*
Mauj - *meaning: joy, pleasure or bliss; in a carefree state.*
*Together the phrase would translate to: This is the
military, not a joyride.*

5. Burnout

(Where are we Headed?)

It's a fast world now,
with growing needs,
High stakes—
Higher rewards...
or so it seems.
At what cost?
Only time will tell.
Me and you—
I know,
It's crude.
And yet, here we **wake, wake, wake**;
In the wee hours, we **break, break, break**
our backs, chasing internet hacks,
choking down breakfast—fast—
with a side of social media trash.
It's hard—
to pull away from this,

when even a minute of peace
feels like bliss,
so we trade silence
for digital noise
in a world
so **harmonious**.
Where's the book-reading?
The soul-searching?
The "I wanna watch a magician"—
Now?
Gone.
Replaced by
Siri, Alexa, Cortana.
Here we go—
Good lord.
That's a drama.
No texts. No calls.
Emails? All false.
Communication?
What's that?
We expect perfection,
but forget how to respond back.
We react—
to the reactions
of others reacting back.
As the dim lights
get dimmer, dimmer, dimmer...

It's time for dinner.
And there are deadlines
to meet.
As we get sucked
into this repeating beat—
this "real world."
They say:
"Go home if you can't get real!"
Real? Ha.
Do they not see
that deadlines
grow dead vines
in the neurons
of our big, bright brains—
triggering hormones
of the *sad kind*,
leaving us all
burnt out,
spaced out,
checked out.
'Nough said?
Yeah?
I'm out.

6. Film Camera

Focus...
Breathe...Click....
Flash!
The stillness of the moment
Captured.
"Perfect"
Timeless, ephemeral.
"Your shots and stories...
I'll send your order in 2 weeks."

A walk; into the dark room
A moment of blind trust
As seasoned hands
Gently spool film onto the reel
A silent and dying art
With no one to teach

As images are re-born
In the light-tight tank
Where past moments become

Present— and held, still and frank,

*"Then comes **timing and temperature,***
To dip the film just right,
Into the chemical bin—
As if nurturing a pulse of light."

Watch invisible light
On the film come alive
As the developing agent
Breathes life
Through care and time

But wait - one must add a fixer
To stop the film from growing still,
So what was once fleeting,
Becomes permanent, by will.

So, as you rinse
and hang dry
the negatives,
A quiet row of sepia stillness,
Waiting to be scanned, developed,
And sent to someone,
As they open—
Flashes, glimpses,
Fragments of life they remembered.

7. Timeline

(To all the 29 year old's with dreams and hopes)

To the girl who isn't following a timeline,
It must be tough to see the signs—
Your friends at 29,
With rings, toys, and love that shines,
All before they even cross that line.

To the girl who isn't following a timeline,
It must sting when family say,
"Look at all your friends today—
Why can't you be like them, eh?
Why take the road that veers astray?"
The pressure must be loud and near—
Their voices echo, sharp and clear:
*"If only you'd done what I said back then,
You'd be so far ahead of them.*

To the girl who isn't following a timeline,
It must feel like hope is thin—

While others climb and cash flows in,
You juggle debts and wear a grin,
Still blamed —and shamed for where you've been.

To the girl who isn't following a timeline,
I promise this with all my might—
You've always had the strength, the fight,
But skill alone won't bend time right,
Nor turn delay to overnight.

So go ahead, keep chasing dreams,
Even if they come in slow, thin streams.
In love, or jobs, or moving out—
Keep walking paths you're sure about.

To the girl who isn't following a timeline—
*You're not behind. You're on **your** time*

8. Ramen

How funny it is, don't you agree?
A veggie like me, seafood-free!
Slurping ramen so joyously,
No meat in sight—just pure ecstasy.

It must be the way they make it,
The chef's quiet heart,
The magic and care—a culinary art.
The broth, so spicy and sweet,
With ssamjang and miso—a savoury treat.

Seared tofu—golden, firm, and light,
And boiled corn—any farmer's delight.
A dish that deserves the crown,
That says, "The heartiest bowl ever found!"

A sprinkle of seaweed, sesame rain,
Might confuse a purist—"This ain't the same!"
But to me, it's ramen through and through—
With every bite, my dreams renew.

Naruto-style, I slurp and sip,
Caught in a manga, bit by bit.
That umami rush in a bowl
Stirs something deep in my desi soul.

Like *rasam rice* from homely days,
It warms me up in familiar ways.
As a college gal, I'd roam and roam,
But ramen brings that taste of home.

9. ANTS: Anxious Negative Thoughts)

Little thoughts that crawl and bite,
Whisper doubts in the dead, quiet night.
They tell me lies I start to trust,
And freeze my limbs with creeping rust.
But I can pause, take one deep breath,
And hush their fear of looming death.
Oh why must they make pit stops —
And make it hard to leave my box —
They're just small anxious and negative thoughts.

10. Matrimonial

They tell me I must marry,
But also say, *"Oh, don't worry,*
There's no such hurry."
But what they refuse to see
Is the 'tea' in society
That often runs without
Modesty.

They tell me I must marry,
And say I must not be picky,
For I will not find a suitor
If my demands – oh dear,
Are too tricky.

They tell me I must marry
To make it easier on my mother,
For I must marry
To carry future progeny,
A duty to no other.

Oh, when will the weight of being
an Asian woman in a society
That bends to rules
And bows to fools – cease?

Till then,
I must not just appease,
But 'be' *Lakshmi, Parvati, and Saraswati.*

In 2025, age 29,
And still I hear, *"Take your time,"*
"Don't worry, there's no rush," they say,
Then hand me profiles, one after the other each day.
With kindness in their eyes,
They persist.

But make no mistake,
There is no force here,
No chains, no hands that bind,
Yet I'm poked at for not being wise enough,
To "trap" a man in time.
So here I stand,
Still relying on arranged plans,
Not married—
Yet still expected to understand.

11. Chariot of Fire

The sun sets low, its warmth retreating,
Drawn by threads the Fates are spinning.
Yet rises still, the vow repeating,
On paths foretold by stars beginning.

In the journey of the Chariot of Fire,
Seven horses race with hearts afire,,
Their path stretches beyond desire,
Their rider - consumed by quagmire.

Loxias seeks his twin with care,
But *Lochia* chose the hush of air.
While she guards the womb, the newborn cries,
He bears the weight of others' rise—
And both still search the endless skies.

He cannot rest, nor turn away,
His path is carved in ancient clay.
Though weary flames burn low by day,

His chariot sways—
The sun must rise; he must obey.

22

Note: *Loxias* and *Lochia* are alternative names used for Apollo and Artemis, respectively, in Greek mythology.

12. Krsna: In the Wake

As darkness engulfs the sky,
Birds fly home, into the night
worms burrow deep,
When all being are asleep
He is awake, he sees.
Into the forests.
He sits atop a Kadamba tree,
Symbolizing eternity.
One breath, and it captivates.
The **bansuri** begins to draw
Animals and human beings across,
Enchanting, Mesmerizing, and Lulling.
Hatred into love - He thaws
A spiritual transcendence unfolds.
The universe to his command, bows.

Note: *Bansuri* is a traditional Indian bamboo flute, often
associated with Lord Krishna.

13. Old Soul

When you are neither born, nor dying,
Merely changing form, undying,
You hold a wisdom beyond your years,
Seeking truth from ancient spheres.
Each cycle of birth, death, and rebirth,
You see through eyes of endless worth,
Like discarding one set of clothes
For another, new life it bestows.
A mentor, keeper of forgotten lore,
Carrying burdens never yours before.
Dear old soul, treat yourself with care,
For many lifetimes you've known despair.
In this life, forgive yourself first,
And let healing begin,
When Osiris calls to weigh your soul,
Against the feather, truth's final toll,
Let go of the cosmic thread that binds,
People, nature, and celestial minds.
Offer the peace you were born to give,
In that peace, may your spirit truly live.

For you've broken free from fate's tight hold,
And the burdens you've carried, now released,
unfold.

Note: *The lines about a mentor, keeper of forgotten lore - reflect the essence of **Chiron**, the wise centaur from Greek mythology. Known as a mentor and healer, Chiron carried the weight of wisdom and knowledge, often guiding heroes like Achilles and Asclepius. Despite his own suffering from an incurable wound, he selflessly imparted forgotten lore and offered counsel, carrying burdens that were never his to bear.*
Note 2: *Osiris is the Egyptian god of the afterlife, death, and resurrection. He symbolizes eternal life and rebirth, ruling the underworld after being resurrected by his wife, Isis.*

14. Formula 1

It's not just metal and tyres—

It's a story told beyond 320 kilometers per hour.

What a flyer!

Understanding it?

Never gender-specific.

Every downshift: a dance with death.

Every overtake: a defiance of physics.

Senna, Schumacher, and Vettel—

The poet in rain, the cold-blooded rebel,

The mind like math, the fire, the level—

Legends who danced on the edge of the gravel.

Verstappen, Leclerc, and Hamilton—

Chaos mastered, the calm, and the champion.

Relentless, refined, and sharp as a talon—

They carve modern myths in full-throttle canon.

Every rev is a heartbeat in the asphalt.

A blitz through Turn 10,
A slice through corners 4 and 7.
These pilots on ground
Live the extreme life—
Milliseconds between trauma and triumph,
The ache of near-misses written into muscle memory.
An F1 car isn't driven.
It is commanded—
Like a tempest obeying a conductor.
As **Ricciardo** once said,
It is "*real sweat.*"
That's what makes a racer.
Who chooses grit over glamour.

15. Ode to the Left-Handed

You praise the gods in ancient lore—
Ambidextrous in battle and art,
Wielding swords with one hand,
And veenas with the other,
Warriors, dancers, singers divine,
Masters of both war and rhyme.

You speak of the valorant Arjuna, steady and sure,
A bow in either hand—
Strings pulled with equal grace,
Arrows loosed from left and right,
Each shot a prayer, each aim divine.
Ambidextrous in war,
He turned the battlefield
Into a dance of mirrored fire,
Graced by gods, fearless in form.

You chant their names in reverence,
Build temples of stone, marble and gold,
Call them mighty, call them blessed—

Balanced hands, balanced souls.

But when your child
Reaches for *rice* with their left,
The music stops.
A hush falls.
Whispers replace hymns.
"Impure," you say.
"Unlearn," you demand.
"Correct it," society chimes.

How fragile your faith must be,
To fear the hand
That mirrors genius, sincerity and authenticity.
The hand **Da Vinci** sketched with,
and **Curie** experimented with,
The hand of difference,
Of daring.

Let them eat with grace,
Let them write, draw, fight,
With the hand that speaks to them.
Let them dance their own rhythm—
A rhythm the gods themselves might envy.

For every left-hander that's born,
A rebellion takes root in flesh,

A reminder that tradition,
When blind,
Needs a gentle nudge—
Or the graceful defiance
Of a firm left-handed blow, in flesh..

16. Fly, Little Butterfly

A small green larva, soft and bright,
Feasts on leaves morning till night.
It munches slow with steady pace,
A quiet life, a hungry grace.
Then off it goes, no need to fight,
To weave its chrysalis snug and tight.
There, it sleeps while time drifts by,
A dreamer soon to touch the sky.
From stillness comes a vibrant flight—
Fly, little butterfly, chase the light.

17. Edinburgh, circa 2017

Amidst the castle, lake, and **Arthur's Seat,**

There was a time we ventured deep—

Through cobbled paths and dusky streets,

It felt, for sure, to be destiny.

In the land of *Arthur, Greyfriars Bobby and Nessie,*

Where tales were thick in the mist and moss,

We lived what now feels like lore, not loss.

For *Auld Lang Syne,*

I write—

In memory of a time

Full of spirits and smiles,

Of tables with takeout *naans,*

And homemade *biryanis and pulaos.*

Movies every second night,

Laughter echoing through the flat—

Dare I say,

A bond unfaded, still burning bright.

We wandered **Dean Village** in silence,

Where **Water of Leith** whispered secrets below,
Strolled by **the Meadows,**
Watched the snow blossom,
On rare weekends,
We escaped to the foot of the
Pentlands Hills—
Allowing the winds braid our thoughts,
Letting the hills know our dreams.

I cherish those moments now,
When things seem amiss.
For they raised some of me—
In learning, in navigating hardship,
In a city that brought joy
Amidst the storm of student life.

I hope and pray
That you all are
Healthy and fine.
Even though we may not talk as often anymore—
Some of you are married, with kids in your arms,
Others, chasing purpose through passion and charm,
And a few of us still meet,
Though it is that moments that are fleeting.

It makes me wonder,
Does one ever find again

Such golden days?
Or are they just encountered—
Rare and a beauty,
Like the Edinburgh unicorn,
Or *Loch Nessie?*

18. Keepsake

Burdened with memories of a lifetime
Long gone,
Enduring—weathered by storms.
They smell of ancient wisdom in the petrichor,
And become nature's silent witness—
With gentle curves and jagged edges.
Some remain grounded, smoothed by time,
Steadfast in moss-covered silence—
Carriers of a distant past
Left behind.

Others venture the seas,
Tucked safely in a pocket,
Below an otter's armpit.
Waiting to be used—a transformation—
A tool to crack open
A clam, or a shell
In the vast, lonely ocean.

Or, if the Otter holds a special memory

With the stone it carries—
Not for the shell it might someday shatter,
But for the weight of the days it has known.
Smoothed by tides, roughened by loss,
It will hold onto it,
Dearly—caressing—
A symbol of everlasting comfort.

19. Pokémon

Once upon a time, in a world so bright,
I watched Pikachu and Ash take flight.
From cartoons to games, I followed along,
A journey of friendship, where we felt we belonged.
Pokéballs in hand, we'd go afar,
Catching creatures, both near and far.
Collecting *Tazos* - spinning with every pack,
Of purple cheetos, a tasty snack.
Adventures were wild, never too small,
Through fields of grass, we'd catch them all.
Defeating *Team Rocket at Celadon*,
With every victory, our bond grew strong.
Friendships evolved with each passing day,
Like a *Charmander* ablaze.
In this world, we learned to rely,
On each other, as we reached for the sky.
Until it was time to close the console,
And get back to the book.
You gotta say we were hooked.
To the fantasy world beyond.

Where dreams took flight - forever fond.
So here's to the days of Pokémon fun,
A reminder that together, we're never undone.

20. Engineered Sunshine

A sweetness too perfect,
Refreshing in the summer heat,
Engineered in a lab—
Brought to me,
A cup of vitamin C.
Rasna—mixed in cold water—
Is the neon citrus glow
Of a concoction
That has never seen
A real orchard grove.
Sweet, sting, and tingle—
With syrupy echoes of fruit,
This lab-born tang,
This so-called fruit,
Brings nostalgia
From the shelf of summer memories—
Sweet,
Because I never questioned it.

21. Cat Dog Base

I adore those whiskered weirdos, and pups with zoomy pace,,
Pets were banned at home—*asthma!*—and the moves we'd always face,
Constantly shifting spots, no time to settle in one place.
"Too risky!" cried my parents, with that worried face,
So now I'm a treat-smuggler, biscuits stuffed in every case.
I dish out love to strays I meet, from metros to under the staircase,
Gossipy neighbors act like I'm leading a furry revolution from base—
Secretly wishing they had my fanbase.
So turn around and - Call me commander of the "Cat-Dog base".
Cause this - is not a phase.